CHURCH GROWTH UNLEASHED
STUDY GUIDE

Copyright © 2024 by Danny Anderson

Published by Arrows & Stones

All rights reserved. No portion of this book may be reproduced, stored in a retrieval system, or transmitted in any form or by any means—electronic, mechanical, photocopy, recording, scanning, or other—except for brief quotations in critical reviews or articles, without prior written permission of the author.

Unless otherwise marked, all Scripture quotations are taken from the Holy Bible, New Living Translation, copyright © 1996, 2004, 2015 by Tyndale House Foundation. Used by permission of Tyndale House Publishers, Inc., Carol Stream, Illinois 60188. All rights reserved. | Scripture quotations marked NIV are taken from the Holy Bible, New International Version®, NIV®. Copyright © 1973, 1978, 1984, 2011 by Biblica, Inc.™ Used by permission of Zondervan. All rights reserved worldwide. www.zondervan.com. The "NIV" and "New International Version" are trademarks registered in the United States Patent and Trademark Office by Biblica, Inc.™ | The ESV® Bible (The Holy Bible, English Standard Version®). ESV® Text Edition: 2016. Copyright © 2001 by Crossway, a publishing ministry of Good News Publishers. The ESV® text has been reproduced in cooperation with and by permission of Good News Publishers. Unauthorized reproduction of this publication is prohibited. All rights reserved. | Scripture quotations marked The Message are taken from THE MESSAGE, copyright © 1993, 1994, 1995, 1996, 2000, 2001, 2002 by Eugene H. Peterson. Used by permission of NavPress. All rights reserved. Represented by Tyndale House Publishers, Inc.

For foreign and subsidiary rights, contact the author.

Cover design by Sara Young

ISBN: 978-1-962401-47-0   1 2 3 4 5 6 7 8 9 10

Printed in the United States of America

STUDY GUIDE
CHURCH GROWTH UNLEASHED

Danny Anderson

ARROWS & STONES

CONTENTS

CHAPTER 1. **YOU NEED TO GROW YOUR CHURCH**...................... 6

CHAPTER 2. **SOUL CARE** 12

CHAPTER 3. **FAMILY** 18

CHAPTER 4. **LEADERSHIP** 24

CHAPTER 5. **PERSEVERANCE** 30

CHAPTER 6. **COMMIT TO CONTINUOUS IMPROVEMENT** 36

CHAPTER 7. **YOUR HEALTH** 42

CHAPTER 8. **THE POWER OF A HOBBY** 48

CHAPTER 9. **DON'T GO ALONE—YOU NEED YOUR FRIENDS** 54

CHURCH GROWTH UNLEASHED

How to Grow Your Church Without Losing Your Soul

Danny Anderson

CHAPTER 1

YOU NEED TO GROW YOUR CHURCH

The church must grow if for no other reason than to counter the bad advice being dished out daily.

READING TIME

As you read Chapter 1: "You Need to Grow Your Church" in *Church Growth Unleashed*, review, reflect on, and respond to the text by answering the following questions.

REVIEW, REFLECT, AND RESPOND

What are some of the dangers of ministry leaders disqualifying themselves?

_____
_____
_____
_____
_____

What is the purpose of the local church? Does your church fulfill this purpose?

_____
_____
_____
_____
_____
_____
_____

Describe the growth of the church as depicted in the book of Acts.

_____
_____
_____
_____
_____
_____

> "And all the believers met together in one place and shared everything they had. They sold their property and possessions and shared the money with those in need. They worshiped together at the Temple each day, met in homes for the Lord's Supper, and shared their meals with great joy and generosity."
>
> —Acts 2:44-46

Consider the scripture above and answer the following questions:

What stands out to you from this passage?

_____
_____
_____
_____
_____
_____
_____
_____

In what ways does your church emulate this description of the early church?

_____
_____
_____

What is conviction, and according to this chapter, why is it so important for pastors?

What analogy does Jesus use in John 4 to describe the difference between physical and spiritual satisfaction?

How does the church provide purpose and meaning for people's lives?

_____
_____
_____
_____
_____
_____

What role does the church play in providing instruction for living?

_____
_____
_____
_____
_____

How important is community within the church, and how does it meet people's needs?

_____
_____
_____
_____
_____

CHAPTER 2
SOUL CARE

Leadership and church growth and inside-out games.

READING TIME

As you read Chapter 2: "Soul Care" in *Church Growth Unleashed*, review, reflect on, and respond to the text by answering the following questions.

REVIEW, REFLECT, AND RESPOND

Considering the analogy of the soul to a car engine, how does the condition of the soul impact a pastor's ability to lead effectively? Discuss the interconnectedness of the mind, emotions, and will, and their influence on ministry outcomes.

_____
_____
_____
_____
_____
_____
_____

Have you ever had your personal value become tied to your church's growth? Why may this be a danger to your congregation?

_____
_____
_____
_____
_____
_____
_____
_____

Drawing from the chapter's exploration of the mind, emotions, and will, how can pastors cultivate a healthier approach to ministry and leadership that prioritizes soul care? Consider practical steps you can take.

_____
_____
_____
_____
_____
_____

> **"And what do you benefit if you gain the whole world but lose your own soul?"**
>
> **—Mark 8:36**

Consider the scripture above and answer the following questions:

How would you define "gain[ing] the whole world"?

_____
_____
_____
_____
_____
_____

What does this verse reveal about soul care?

___

Reflect on your own priorities as a pastor. Are there areas where you find yourself sacrificing important aspects of life, such as family time, personal health, or spiritual well-being, for the sake of ministry results? How can you identify and address any imbalances in your life?

___

Consider the stresses you face in ministry. How do you currently cope with stress, and are these methods healthy and sustainable in the long term?

_____
_____
_____
_____
_____
_____
_____
_____
_____

Evaluate your current practices regarding soul care rhythms, such as daily quiet time, weekly Sabbath, quarterly breaks, and yearly vacations. Which of these rhythms are you currently prioritizing, and which ones might require more attention? How can you begin implementing or improving these practices in your life and ministry?

_____
_____
_____
_____
_____
_____
_____
_____
_____

Describe how a healthy soul influences your motives, decision-making, relationships with your team and congregation, and overall leadership style. How can prioritizing soul care enhance your leadership impact and create a healthier ministry environment?

_____
_____
_____
_____
_____
_____
_____
_____
_____
_____
_____

CHAPTER 3

FAMILY

The health of your church will not exceed the health of your marriage.

REVIEW, REFLECT, AND RESPOND

READING TIME

As you read Chapter 3: "Family" in *Church Growth Unleashed*, review, reflect on, and respond to the text by answering the following questions.

What is the importance of prioritizing family over church responsibilities for pastors?

_____
_____
_____
_____
_____

What are some reasons pastors tend to put the church first, according to this chapter? Have you ever been guilty of this?

_____
_____
_____
_____
_____
_____
_____

Why is it important for pastors to see their family as their closest teammates in ministry? Do you do this?

_____
_____
_____
_____
_____
_____

> **"If a man does not know how to rule his own house, how will he take care of the church of God?"**
>
> —1 Timothy 3:5 (NKJV)

Consider the scripture above and answer the following questions:

What is the meaning of this scripture?

_____
_____
_____
_____
_____
_____
_____
_____

How does this verse speak to your priorities?

_____
_____
_____
_____
_____
_____
_____
_____

What practical steps can you take to put your family first while still growing your church?

_____
_____
_____
_____
_____
_____
_____
_____
_____
_____

How do scheduling conflicts between church and family activities impact the family dynamic, according to this chapter? Describe a time you have experienced this.

_____
_____
_____
_____
_____
_____
_____
_____
_____
_____

Do you have a weekly date night with your spouse? Why or why not?

_____
_____
_____
_____
_____
_____
_____
_____
_____
_____

What is the difference between a vacation and a trip, in the context of family time?

_____
_____
_____
_____
_____
_____
_____
_____
_____
_____
_____

How does incorporating an evening bedtime ritual contribute to the spiritual development of a pastor's family? How can you incorporate this into your family?

___

CHAPTER 4

LEADERSHIP

A big reason why so many leaders struggle is because they don't fully understand the four critical functions of leadership.

READING TIME

As you read Chapter 4: "Leadership" in *Church Growth Unleashed*, review, reflect on, and respond to the text by answering the following questions.

REVIEW, REFLECT, AND RESPOND

What are the four critical functions of leadership according to the chapter, and why are they important for effectively leading a church? Which of these four functions do you struggle with the most?

_____
_____
_____
_____
_____
_____
_____
_____

Based on this chapter, what does it take to effectively cast a compelling vision for a church? Have you done this?

_____
_____
_____
_____
_____
_____
_____
_____

> "But now [Nehemiah] said to them, 'You know very well what trouble we are in. Jerusalem lies in ruins, and its gates have been destroyed by fire. Let us rebuild the wall of Jerusalem and end this disgrace!'"
>
> —Nehemiah 2:17

Consider the scripture above and answer the following questions:

What stands out to you from this passage about Nehemiah's leadership?

_____
_____
_____
_____
_____
_____
_____

How effectively did Nehemiah share his vision through this statement?

_____
_____
_____
_____
_____
_____
_____

Discuss the importance of communicating the "why" behind the vision for a church. Why is it necessary for leaders to articulate the reasons for their objectives?

_____
_____
_____
_____
_____
_____
_____
_____
_____
_____
_____

Explain the difference between external and internal church growth strategies, and provide examples of each from the chapter or your own experience. Which of these strategies can your church implement?

_____
_____
_____
_____
_____
_____
_____
_____
_____
_____
_____

Why is building a strong team so crucial for the success of a church's vision? What characteristics should leaders look for when assembling their leadership team?

_____
_____
_____
_____
_____
_____
_____
_____
_____

Discuss the concept of giving away power as a leader. Why is it essential, and what potential benefits does it offer for church growth and development? Who have you given away power to?

_____
_____
_____
_____
_____
_____
_____
_____
_____

Take time to create a 90-day rhythm for goal-setting and execution within a church leadership team, as outlined in this chapter.

What are the four key elements of a weekly leadership meeting, and how do they contribute to maintaining focus, accountability, and problem-solving within a church leadership team? Are these elements present in your weekly leadership meeting?

CHAPTER 5

PERSEVERANCE

Pastor, if you want to grow your church and reach people with the gospel, there is pain ahead. But the pain has a purpose—your growth.

REDING TIME

As you read Chapter 5: "Perseverance" in *Church Growth Unleashed*, review, reflect on, and respond to the text by answering the following questions.

REVIEW, REFLECT, AND RESPOND

What does this chapter identify as the "real problems" that shake leaders to their core and cause them to doubt their abilities? Have you ever encountered any of these?

_____
_____
_____
_____
_____
_____
_____
_____

What is the common denominator for all leaders of healthy, growing churches?

_____
_____
_____
_____
_____
_____
_____
_____

Explain the concept of "embracing pain" as discussed in the chapter and why it's essential for pastors. Do you effectively embrace pain?

_____
_____
_____
_____
_____
_____

> **"We were crushed and overwhelmed beyond our ability to endure, and we thought we would never live through it. In fact, we expected to die. But as a result, we stopped relying on ourselves and learned to rely on God, who raises the dead."**
>
> **—2 Corinthians 1:8-9**

Consider the scripture above and answer the following questions:

What stands out to you from this passage of scripture?

_____
_____
_____
_____
_____

What do these verses reveal about true perseverance?

_____
_____
_____
_____
_____
_____
_____

Describe a personal experience that illustrates the concept of embracing pain and trusting in God's provision.

_____
_____
_____
_____
_____
_____
_____

Provide examples of lessons that you have learned by going through difficulty.

_____
_____
_____
_____
_____
_____
_____

According to this chapter, what opportunity does pain always present, and how should pastors approach it?

_____
_____
_____
_____
_____
_____
_____
_____
_____
_____

Reflecting on the chapter, what are some actionable steps you can take to build your capacity to endure pain and grow through difficulties in ministry?

_____
_____
_____
_____
_____
_____
_____
_____
_____
_____
_____
_____

CHAPTER 6

COMMIT TO CONTINUOUS IMPROVEMENT

You know that your church is beginning to value vision over preference when you can let go of things that have run their course.

READING TIME

As you read Chapter 6: "Commit to Continuous Improvement" in *Church Growth Unleashed*, review, reflect on, and respond to the text by answering the following questions.

REVIEW, REFLECT, AND RESPOND

How did Michael Jordan's commitment to continuous improvement contribute to his success in basketball?

_____
_____
_____
_____
_____
_____
_____
_____

Why do pastors and churches often struggle to implement necessary improvements? Have you struggled in this field?

_____
_____
_____
_____
_____
_____
_____
_____
_____

What are some common reasons why people resist change in the church environment? Have you experienced this?

___

> **"Yes, I try to find common ground with everyone, doing everything I can to save some. I do everything to spread the Good News and share in its blessings."**
>
> —1 Corinthians 9:22-23

Consider the scripture above and answer the following questions:

What stands out to you from this passage?

___

What does this verse reveal about sharing the gospel?

_____
_____
_____
_____
_____
_____
_____

What are the key elements of staying current and relevant in church ministry? Do you need to work on implementing any of these?

_____
_____
_____
_____
_____
_____
_____

How can your church exceed the low expectations of those who have had negative experiences with church in the past?

_____
_____
_____
_____
_____
_____
_____

Why is continuous learning essential for pastors and church leaders? How do you practice this?

_____
_____
_____
_____
_____
_____
_____
_____
_____
_____

Provide examples of how churches can learn and improve from sources outside of their own organization.

_____
_____
_____
_____
_____
_____
_____
_____
_____
_____
_____

What does it mean to value the vision over preferences in church ministry?

_____
_____
_____
_____
_____
_____
_____
_____
_____
_____
_____
_____
_____
_____

CHAPTER 7

YOUR HEALTH

Sometimes I wonder if poor physical health is not only the reason why pastors quit but perhaps also the catalyst for some of the other reasons.

READING TIME

As you read Chapter 7: "Your Health in *Church Growth Unleashed*, review, reflect on, and respond to the text by answering the following questions.

REVIEW, REFLECT, AND RESPOND

What health statistics shared in this chapter stick out to you? Are you a part of any of these statistics?

_____
_____
_____
_____
_____
_____
_____
_____

How is a pastor's physical health connected to the growth of their church? Have you ever experienced this to be true in your church?

_____
_____
_____
_____
_____
_____
_____
_____
_____
_____

How might poor physical health contribute to other reasons pastors leave the ministry?

_____
_____
_____
_____

> "Don't you realize that your body is the temple of the Holy Spirit, who lives in you and was given to you by God? You do not belong to yourself, for God bought you with a high price. So you must honor God with your body."
>
> —1 Corinthians 6:19-20

Consider the scripture above and answer the following questions:

How does this verse affect your perception of your body and health?

_____
_____
_____
_____
_____
_____
_____

What do you think it means to honor God with your body?

___

What are the four reasons given in this chapter for pastors to value their physical health?

___

What is the importance of setting an example of physical health for the congregation? Do you do this currently?

___

What are the key priorities given for maintaining physical health?

___

Do you surround yourself with healthy individuals? Why may this be beneficial?

___

What practical actions can you take in the coming days, weeks, and months to improve your health?

_____
_____
_____
_____
_____
_____
_____
_____
_____
_____
_____
_____
_____
_____

CHAPTER 8

THE POWER OF A HOBBY

The "I'm too busy" excuse is one of two things: it's either an overvaluing of one's importance or a failure in leadership to develop a team and empower others.

READING TIME

As you read Chapter 8: "The Power of a Hobby" in *Church Growth Unleashed*, review, reflect on, and respond to the text by answering the following questions.

REVIEW, REFLECT, AND RESPOND

What are some of the potential dangers of allowing ministry work to consume your life? Have you ever been a victim of these dangers?

_____
_____
_____
_____
_____
_____

Do you find it difficult to fully disconnect from ministry to engage in a hobby? If so, why do you think this is?

_____
_____
_____
_____
_____
_____

What hobbies do you have, if any? What hobbies interest you?

_____
_____
_____
_____
_____

> **You keep him in perfect peace
> whose mind is stayed on you,
> because he trusts in you.**
>
> —Isaiah 26:3

Consider the scripture above and answer the following questions:

What does it mean to have one's mind "stayed on" God?

_____
_____
_____
_____
_____
_____
_____
_____

How might engaging in a hobby indicate that you have complete trust in God?

_____
_____
_____
_____
_____
_____
_____

In what ways can engaging in a hobby help pastors manage stress and avoid burnout?

According to this chapter, how can a hobby give pastors a sense of control and completion in their lives?

What role do hobbies play in helping pastors develop friendships?

How does engaging in a hobby help pastors feel like normal people and break down perceptions of being solely focused on ministry?

Speak to the importance of prioritizing hobbies and not feeling guilty about taking time for them. Is this a challenge for you?

___
___
___
___
___
___
___
___
___
___
___
___

CHAPTER 9

DON'T GO ALONE— YOU NEED YOUR FRIENDS

As it turns out, we need friendships as much as we need anything else to stay healthy.

READING TIME

As you read Chapter 9: "Don't Go Alone–You Need Your Friends" in *Church Growth Unleashed*, review, reflect on, and respond to the text by answering the following questions.

REVIEW, REFLECT, AND RESPOND

How does the Bible illustrate the importance of friendship in David's life?

_____
_____
_____
_____
_____
_____
_____
_____
_____

What is one of the characteristics of effective pastors, according to this chapter? Do you possess this trait?

_____
_____
_____
_____
_____
_____
_____
_____
_____

> **"Jonathan went to find David and encouraged him to stay strong in his faith in God."**
>
> —1 Samuel 23:16

Consider the scripture above and answer the following questions:

What does this verse reveal about friendships?

_____
_____
_____
_____
_____
_____
_____

Who do you have in your life that can encourage you like Jonathan did to David?

_____
_____
_____
_____
_____
_____
_____

What unique challenges do pastors face in developing and maintaining friendships? Have you ever experienced these challenges?

What potential pitfalls can arise when pastors develop friendships with congregants?

According to Dietrich Bonhoeffer, what is the significance of the physical presence of other Christians in the context of friendship?

_____
_____
_____
_____
_____
_____
_____
_____
_____

What friendships do you have that can provide you with insight and strength to navigate the challenges of ministry?

_____
_____
_____
_____
_____
_____
_____
_____
_____

www.ingramcontent.com/pod-product-compliance
Lightning Source LLC
Chambersburg PA
CBHW062123080426
42734CB00012B/2963